CW01635094

Dr. D. K. Olukoya

# The Problem of Bewitched Hands and Feet

Dr D.K. Olukoya

The problem of bewitched hands and feet



A publication of
mountain of fire and miracles ministries
13. Olasimbo Street. off Olumo Road. Onike,
P. O. Box 2990, Sabo, Yaba, Lagos, Nigeria.

ISBN: 978-978-920-002-3



For further information or permission contact:
Email: pasteurdanielolukova french@vahoo.fr
mfmhqworldwide@mountainoffire.org

Or visit our website: yww mountmountainoffire.org
http:y/mfmbilingualbooks4evangelism.blogspot,com/

Psalm 144:1: "Blessed be the LORD my strength, which teacheth my hands to war, and my fingers to fight".

This means that your hands are weapons and they can fight the war of your life. War can be raised against your hands. You might not know it but the enemy sees your hands as an instrument of war.

Deuteronomy 28:20: "*The LORD shall send upon thee cursing, vexation, and rebuke, in all that thou settest thine hand unto for to do, until thou be destroyed, and until thou perish quickly; because of the wickedness of thy doings, whereby thou hast forsaken me*".

This means that the hand can be a subject of cursing, vexation, or of rebuke in order to ruin a person.

Romans 10:15: "*And how shall they preach, except they be sent? As it is written: "How beautiful are the feet of them that preach the gospel of peace, and bring glad tidings of good things!"*"

This means that if someone with the gospel of peace enters into an arena, joy and peace enters into that arena. The opposite too holds true; that is to say that some feet are ugly.

I would like you to carefully read this book, as if you are studying a mathematical subject and pray the prayers with all the determination that you can gather. Many things are going to happen, as far as you pray fervently. A man is a spirit living in a body and having a soul. If the spirit man of a person is called out of him or her that spirit will look exactly like the person, in form and shape but it will not have the human body. The spirit man will have hands, legs, everything that the human being has. Every organ in the body physically, has a spiritual representative.

Each organ that is in the body physically has a spiritual significance and symbol. For example, the head in the spirit is the symbol of your destiny. The legs are the symbol of movement and it means that if the legs are tied spiritually, it does not mean that the person will not move around but that person will not make any progress. If the hands of a person are tied spiritually, the person could be beating drums and fighting all about or cook, nothing good will come out of it. The hands in the spirit represent a person's labour; or handiwork. Every other organ of the body has a representative in the spirit realm. When good people enter into the life of a person, good things happen. When wrong things enter into the life of a person, wrong things happen. When wrong people get out of a person's life, good things begin to happen. Many people do not know when the connection of some people to their life, is over; they stick to people that they should actually chase out of their lives, because their contribution to such a destiny is over. When God has already said they should go and you continue to let them stay, trouble starts.

Take these prayer points with all the seriousness that you can gather:
- Every evil foot that has entered into my life, jump out by fire, in the Name of Jesus.
- Every evil hand that is upon the affairs of my life, wither by fire, in the Name of Jesus.

One very good example is Joseph. Immediately he entered into the house of Portiphar, all that Portiphar did prospered. Everything that Joseph laid his hand upon to do, prospered; flourished and multiplied. I pray that God will send a 'Joseph' into your house and your business and career, in the Name of Jesus. The house of Portiphar prospered because Joseph an employee was there. If you employ the wrong person, somebody with a cursed or bewitched hand trouble will start. A couple prayed for about eighteen years, to have a child and then had one. They employed a house-help from the village and one day, she was playing with the baby; she threw him up in order to grasp him in mid-air but she had forgotten that there was a fan in the ceiling, which was rolling at top speed. Before she knew what was happening, the baby had dropped dead.

I pray and it is a serious prayer; that if there is any evil hand in your destiny now, by the power of the God of Elijah, it shall be cut off in the Name of Jesus.

Your hand is an instrument of power-transfer; that is why men of God lay hands on people. Your hand is a carrier of honour and can transfer blessings to anything you touch. Your hand is the key to your increase and prosperity and can be a symbol of victory in warfare. That is the mystery of Moses' stay on the mountain and Aaron and Ur, had to uphold his hands, Whenever they relented and his hand came down, the Israelites that were on the battle- field, began to lose but when his hand was up, they won the battle. I pray that any power that wants to pull down your hand of victory shall be destroyed today, in the Name of Jesus.

Your hand can build a palace for you here on earth; your hand is the instrument of deliverance and key to defeating your enemies; it is your instrument of healing.

Mark 1617-18: "*And these signs shall follow them that believe; in my name shall they cast out devils; they shall speak with new tongues; they shall take up serpents; and if they drink any deadly thing, it shall not hurt them; they shall lay hands on the sick, and they shall recover*".

When you begin to notice cobwebs around your hands physically or spiritually, it means they have been bewitched. This is one of our reasons for not wedding couples with rings at MFM. It is possible for a ring to be manipulated by evil doers and it will work against the marriage. It could be an ordinary handshake; just to have contact with the ring. They can bewitch that ring which you and your husband have used in making a covenant. That is why we wed with the Holy Bible; the word of God, which cannot be broken or bewitched. Nothing can be done against the word of God; we have to be very careful.

One day, a woman travelled by air for a conference and she lodged in a hotel. Before she went to bed, she removed her wedding and engagement rings and placed them on the bed-side table in the room. Someone came into the room without her knowledge, to exchange the rings for another pair which looked exactly the same way. She did not know that anything had happened and so, after taking her bath, she put on the rings again. Shortly afterwards, that same morning, she received a phone call from her husband who said she should find herself another husband from the conference and not come back to his house. She thought it was a joke because he was the one who took her to the airport as she was leaving the previous day. The reality of her problem dawned on her when she heard the voice of a woman laughing in the background. If you find out that as soon as you got married, you or your spouse lost his or her job; there is bewitchment around the corner. If you find out that you get a lot of money but it disappears mysteriously, your hands have been bewitched and they need deliverance.

Many years ago, a pastor was running some people through deliverance and a huge amount of money was brought into the church premises and locked up in a room.

When the Pastor got there, the money had disappeared. Since the door was locked he knew that nobody went into the room so. He started to pray. Suddenly, the Spirit of God ministered to him that the culprit was one of the deliverance candidates. He went straight to him and asked what he had done and the person confessed that he pulled out the money with the aid of a spiritual needle which he coughed out of his mouth. It was four times that size of a normal needle. By the time he had finished confessing, the culprit asked the pastor to go back and check the money and it was intact. This is to illustrate the fact that money can be spiritually stolen.

When you dream of being chained or you appear before a satanic panel of judges, or you have an evil document in your hand, it is trouble. When you notice that anything you lay your hands upon to do, does not prosper; or works for some time and then collapses, and then there is trouble many years ago, a woman had a prosperous restaurant near the university campus suddenly; she noticed that her business was no longer prospering. She started to pray and the Lord made her to know that the girl that was helping her in the kitchen had strange powers. She found out that once the girl touched the spoon, the stew would go sour. Customers complained and stopped patronising her, but that woman tried to convince them that she just finished cooking, until she tasted it, yet she did not know how it became sour until the Lord exposed the girl. If you find out that you have tried all kinds of trades and professions but nothing worked, then your hands have been bewitched and must be delivered. If you find out that you are very energetic and can really work hard but you do not prosper in anything, then your hands need deliverance. If you notice that you are strong, intelligent but cannot find a befitting job or trade, your hands have been polluted. If you find it difficult to gather money, you have tried many trades, but things still seem not to be what you expect, you are under attack of bewitching powers.

Beloved, I would like you to understand this message and be prepared to pray very well. Sometimes, problems come when you have used your hands to shed innocent blood or you have received bribes from people. Bewitchment will also arise because of curse from God. If you have incisions on your hands, or you have allowed your fingernails to be used for rituals, or you have contributed money towards village rituals and sacrifices, bewitchment can arise. If you give your money to someone who has been cursed by God himself, it will make you a cursed person.

The feet are the instrument of dominion. The Bible says you shall tread upon serpents and scorpions and upon every power of the enemy and nothing shall by any means hurt you. In the spirit, your feet are a symbol of dominion. If they are bewitched, you have a serious problem at hand. A single person with bewitched feet can put all the passengers in a vehicle into serious trouble. The vehicle could be involved in an accident which would claim lives.

A sister boarded an aircraft and they had a stop-over somewhere and the Lord ministered to her that some eaters of flesh and drinkers of blood had just boarded the plane. The Lord told her that she should start praying and that she should not eat the food that she had been given. The sister did not take the message seriously and she ate her food. Suddenly, there was high turbulence; the pilot expressed his sincere regrets and told the passengers that he did not know their destination. He had lost his bearing; the aircraft had turned upside down. He asked the passengers to start praying to the *Supreme Being* that each of them believed in. People started to cry; it was then that the sister realized her mistake and started to pray. She prayed until she started to prophesy that there would be no crash. The Lord answered her prayers and they landed safely. When they arrived, she confessed that she had never in her life, prayed the way she did on that day. All these because some evil feet got into the aircraft.

Your feet are the key to your possession. There is room for the possession of all your benefits. You have a right in the world to walk in and possessed all what belongs to you. However, if your feet are bewitched possessing your possession will be a serious problem. Your feet are meant to establish your breakthroughs and if they are in trouble, it means you too are in trouble. Your feet are an instrument of direction, greatness, deliverance, expansion and blessings. Your feet are weapons of warfare that help you to overcome. The bible says, how beautiful are the feet of them that preach the Gospel of peace, that bring glad tidings of great joy.

The Bible says that there was joy in Samaria when Philip entered into the city. I met a man in the United Kingdom, who was 42 years old. By that time, he had proposed to 21 ladies and they had all turned him down. He just found out that whenever a relationship started, the lady would come after two or three days and end it; she would even ban him from getting in touch with her again. When he started to pray for the deliverance of the feet his situation changed. Do you notice that you always walk into trouble and it is God that has been saving you from terrible accidents? You need to pray hard today, so that your feet can be delivered. Do you notice that whenever there is opportunity for you to receive breakthroughs, honour or blessings, you always get there late? Do you notice that sometimes you walk into disappointments?

Do you notice a lack of breakthrough in spite of all your efforts? Are your helpers always being attacked? Do you notice that sometimes, when you walk into a place, people do not want to see you at all? It is evidence that your feet need some attention.

We live in a wicked environment. A brother got to his shop one day and suddenly felt cold sensation on his foot. He looked down and found out that he had dipped his foot in a pot of sacrifice placed right in front of his shop. There are people who remove sand from the foot-prints of others, in order to use it for charms against them. Some wicked people carve effigies to represent others and then knock nails into the hands or legs or any part of the body, where they want to afflict that person. Today, the Lord wants to get such people free.

## WHAT TO DO

1. You need to repent, confess and forsake your sins, accept the Lord Jesus Christ into your life as your personal Lord and Saviour.

2. Command the bewitchment on your hands and feet to be broken. This is because many people are bound in the spirit, but they do not know.

There was a woman, who was curved, that went to the temple every day. None knew that she was bound until the Lord Jesus Christ came her way. By the time Jesus looked he said, Woman, thou art loosed!
Many people today have their spirit-man bound with ropes or chains. Such people do not make progress in life; they face attacks

from every angle and on every area of their destiny. I am very certain beloved that as you are reading this message and as you pray the prayers with the whole of your being today will be like your birthday, in the name of Jesus. Today will mark beginning of great things in your life, in the mighty name of Jesus.

However, if you have not yet surrendered your life to the Lord Jesus Christ, you are not born again, I would like you to do so right there where you are. All you need do is to recognize and acknowledge that fact that you are a sinner and that you cannot approach God in your sinful state. You need to cry unto the Lord; confess your sins to Him; name them one after the other and ask Him to forgive you and cleanse you from all unrighteousness. Claim the redemptive power in the blood of Jesus that was shed on the cross at Calvary, for the redemption of your life.

Renounce the world and the devil and make sure you do not go back to them again. Invite the Lord Jesus into your life ask Him to come into your life and be your personal Lord and saviour. Hand over the affairs of your life and all that concerns you. Say bye-bye to the devil and enter into the kingdom of light.

I congratulate you on the decision that you have just taken. It is the most important decision in life and l pray that it shall be permanent in your life in the name of Jesus. My prayer for you is that the Lord will take control of your life and keep you from falling. I pray that your name will be written in the Book of life and you will not rub it off, in the name of Jesus. Now examine your life, see if there is any sin that will detain, delay or destroy your deliverance today. It is important for you to do it from the bottom of your heart, so that the angle of your blessings will not pass you by. Now take these prayer points with all the aggression that you can gather.

**PRAYER POINTS**

1. Every power tying down my spirit man, release me and die by fire in the name of Jesus.

2. Every power bewitching my hands die in the name of Jesus.

3. Every power bewitching my feet die in the name of Jesus.

4. Let God arise and make me shine in the name of Jesus.

5. My stolen destiny, I repossess you by fire in the name of Jesus.

6. Every evil pattern of destiny in my family line, my life is not your candidate die, in the name of Jesus.

7. Every witchcraft power that has refused to let me go, I bury you now in the name of Jesus.

8. Every agenda of stubborn pursuers in my life die in the name of Jesus.

9. I fire back every arrow of oppressor in my life, in the name of Jesus.

10. Every altar of witchcraft in my life, come out and die in the name of Jesus.

11. Every opportunity to become extra-ordinary in all areas of life locate me now by fire in the name of Jesus.

12. O eagle of my life, fly to the highest in the name of Jesus.

13. Everywhere I have been denied access, I enter you by fire in the mighty name of Jesus.

14. O God of Jabez change my situation today in Jesus today in the name of Jesus.

15. Every enemy of my greatness in life, scatter in the name mighty name of Jesus.

16. Opportunities to make it physically and spiritually, locate me by fire in the name of Jesus.

17. Heaven of my breakthroughs open by fire in Jesus name.

18. The joy in my heart reject bewitchment in the name of Jesus.

19. O God arise and bring me into my place of blessings in the name of Jesus.

20. Every curse of limitation die in the mighty name of Jesus.

## ABOUT D. K. OLUKOYA

Dr. D. K. Olukoya is the General Overseer of the Mountain of Fire and Miracles Ministries and the Battle Cry Ministries. He holds a First Class Honours Degree in Microbiology from the University of Lagos, Nigeria and a Ph.D. in Molecular Genetics from the University of Reading, United Kingdom. As a researcher, he has over eighty scientific publications to his credit. Anointed by God, Dr. Olukoya is a teacher, prophet, evangelist and preacher of the word. His life and that of his wife, Shade and their son, Elijah Toluwani, are living proofs that all power belongs to God.

## ABOUT MOUNTAIN OF FIRE AND MIRACLES MINISTRIES

Mountain of Fire and Miracles Ministries, is a ministry devoted to the revival of apostolic signs, Holy Ghost fireworks and the unlimited demonstration of the power of God to deliver to the uttermost. Absolute holiness within and without, as the greatest spiritual insecticide, and a condition for heaven is taught openly. MFM is a do-it-yourself Gospel Ministry, where your hands are trained to wage war and your fingers to fight.

A brief history of Mountain of Fire and Miracles Ministries Incorporated
The Mountain of Fire and Miracles was founded in 1989. The first meeting was held at the home of Dr. D. K Olukoya and had 24

persons in attendance. The Church later moved to No. 60, Old Yaba Road, Lagos, and then to the present International Headquarters, site on 24th April, 1994. The Mountain of Fire and Miracles Ministries' Headquarters is the largest single Christian congregation in Africa, with attendance of over 200,000 in single meetings. Mountain of Fire and Miracles Ministries is a full gospel ministry devoted to the revival of apostolic signs, Holy Ghost fireworks and the unlimited demonstration of the power of God to deliver to the uttermost. Absolute holiness, within and without, as the greatest spiritual insecticide and a pre-requisite for heaven is taught openly. MFM is a do-it-yourself Gospel ministry, where your hands are trained to wage war and your fingers to do battle.

16717361R00019

Printed in Great Britain
by Amazon